Flowers for Hitler

●

A NOTE ON THE TITLE

A
while ago
this book would
have been called
SUNSHINE FOR NAPOLEON,
and earlier still it
would have been
called
WALLS FOR GENGHIS KHAN

LEONARD
COHEN

•

Flowers
for
Hitler

•

•

MCCLELLAND AND STEWART
LIMITED
TORONTO/MONTREAL

© COPYRIGHT
Leonard Cohen, 1964

Second printing, August 1966

ALL RIGHTS RESERVED
No part of this book
may be reproduced in any form
without permission in writing
from the publishers,
except by a reviewer
who may quote brief passages
in a review to be printed
in a magazine or newspaper.

The Canadian Publishers
McClelland and Stewart Limited
25 Hollinger Road, Toronto 16

DESIGN: F. NEWFELD

PRINTED AND BOUND
IN ENGLAND BY
HAZELL WATSON & VINEY LTD

CONTENTS

13. What I'm Doing Here
14. The Hearth
15. Portrait of the City Hall
15. Congratulations
16. The Drawer's Condition on November 28, 1961
17. The Suit
18. Business as Usual
19. Indictment of the Blue Hole
20. Nothing I Can Lose
21. Police Gazette
22. No Partners
23. On the Death of an Uncharted Planet
24. I Wanted to Be a Doctor
25. On Hearing a Name Long Unspoken
26. Finally I Called
27. Style
28. Goebbels Abandons His Novel and Joins the Party
30. Why Commands Are Obeyed
31. It Uses Us!
32. The First Murder
33. My Teacher is Dying
35. Montreal 1964
36. Why Experience Is No Teacher
36. For My Old Layton
38. The Only Tourist in Havana Turns His Thoughts Homeward
39. The Invisible Trouble
40. Sick Alone
41. Millennium
43. Hitler the Brain-Mole

- 43. Death of a Leader
- 45. Alexander Trocchi, Public Junkie, Priez Pour Nous
- 48. Three Good Nights
- 50. To a Man Who Thinks He Is Making an Angel
- 51. On the Sickness of My Love
- 52. Cruel Baby
- 52. For Marianne
- 53. The Failure of a Secular Life
- 54. My Mentors
- 54. Hydra 1960
- 55. Leviathan
- 56. Heirloom
- 57. Promise
- 58. Sky
- 59. Waiting for Marianne
- 59. Why I Happen to Be Free
- 61. The True Desire
- 62. The Way Back
- 63. The Project
- 65. Hydra 1963
- 66. All There Is to Know about Adolph Eichmann
- 67. The New Leader
- 68. How It Happened in the Middle of the Day
- 69. For E.J.P.
- 70. The Glass Dog
- 72. A Migrating Dialogue
- 74. The Bus
- 75. Laundry
- 76. The Rest Is Dross
- 77. How the Winter Gets In
- 78. Propaganda
- 78. Opium and Hitler
- 80. For Anyone Dressed in Marble
- 80. Wheels, Fireclouds

81.	Folk
81.	I Had It for a Moment
83.	Island Bulletin
84.	Independence
85.	The House
86.	Order
87.	Destiny
88.	Queen Victoria and Me
89.	The Pure List and the Commentary
91.	The New Step (A Ballet-Drama in One Act)
105.	The Paper
106.	Nursery Rhyme
107.	Old Dialogue
107.	Winter Bulletin
108.	Why Did You Give My Name to the Police?
110.	Governments Make Me Lonely
111.	The Lists
112.	To the Indian Pilgrims
113.	The Music Crept By Us
114.	The Telephone
116.	Disguises
119.	Lot
120.	One of the Nights I Didn't Kill Myself
121.	The Big World
121.	Narcissus
122.	Cherry Orchards
123.	Streetcars
124.	Bullets
125.	Hitler
126.	Front Lawn
127.	Kerensky
128.	Another Night with Telescope

FOR MARIANNE

If from the inside of the Lager, a message could have seeped out to free men, it would have been this: Take care not to suffer in your own homes what is inflicted on us here.

PRIMO LEV

WHAT I'M DOING HERE

I do not know if the world has lied
I have lied
I do not know if the world has conspired against love
I have conspired against love
The atmosphere of torture is no comfort
I have tortured
Even without the mushroom cloud
still I would have hated
Listen
I would have done the same things
even if there were no death
I will not be held like a drunkard
under the cold tap of facts
I refuse the universal alibi

Like an empty telephone booth passed at night
and remembered
like mirrors in a movie palace lobby consulted
only on the way out
like a nymphomaniac who binds a thousand
into strange brotherhood
I wait
for each one of you to confess

THE HEARTH

The day wasn't exactly my own
since I checked
    and found it on a public calendar.
Tripping over many pairs of legs
as I walked down the park
    I also learned my lust
was not so rare a masterpiece.

Buildings actually built
wars planned with blood and fought
men who rose to generals
    deserved an honest thought
as I walked down the park.

I came back quietly to your house
which has a place on a street.
    Not a single other house
disappeared when I came back.
You said some suffering
    had taught me that.

I'm slow to learn I began
to speak of stars and hurricanes.
    Come here little Galileo –
you undressed my vision –
    *it's happier and easier by far
or cities wouldn't be so big.*

Later you worked over lace
    and I numbered many things
your fingers and all fingers did.
As if to pay me a sweet
    for my ardour on the rug
you wondered in the middle of a stitch:
Now what about those stars and hurricanes?

PORTRAIT OF THE CITY HALL

    The diamonds of guilt
    The scrolls of guilt
    The pillars of guilt
    The colours of guilt
    The flags of guilt
    The gargoyles of guilt
    The spines of guilt

Listen, says the mayor, listen to the woodland birds,
They are singing like men in chains.

CONGRATULATIONS

Here we are eating the sacred mushrooms
out of the Japanese heaven
eating the flower
in the sands of Nevada

Hey Marco Polo
and you Arthur Rimbaud
friends of the sailing craft
examine our time's adventure
the jewelled house of Dachau
Belsen's drunk fraternity

Don't your boats seem
like floating violins
playing Jack Benny tunes?

THE DRAWER'S CONDITION
ON NOVEMBER 28, 1961

Is there anything emptier
than the drawer where
you used to store your opium?
How like a blackeyed susan
blinded into ordinary daisy
is my pretty kitchen drawer!
How like a nose sans nostrils
is my bare wooden drawer!
How like an eggless basket!
How like a pool sans tortoise!
My hand has explored
my drawer like a rat
in an experiment of mazes.
Reader, I may safely say
there's not an emptier drawer
in all of Christendom!

THE SUIT

I am locked in a very expensive suit
old elegant and enduring
Only my hair has been able to get free
but someone has been leaving
their dandruff in it
Now I will tell you
all there is to know about optimism
Each day in hub cap mirror
in soup reflection
in other people's spectacles
I check my hair
for an army of alpinists
for Indian rope trick masters
for tangled aviators
for dove and albatross
for insect suicides
for abominable snowmen
I check my hair
for aerialists of every kind
Dedicated as an automatic elevator
I comb my hair for possibilities
I stick my neck out
I lean illegally from locomotive windows
and only for the barber
do I wear a hat

BUSINESS AS USUAL

The gold roof of Parliament covered
with fingerprints and scratches.
And here are the elected, hunchbacked
from climbing on each other's heads.

The most precious secret has been leaked:
There is no Opposition!

Over-zealous hacks hoist the P.M.
through the ceiling. He fools
an entire sled-load of Miss Canada losers
by acting like a gargoyle.

Some fool (how did he get in) who
wants jobs for everyone and says
so in French is quickly interred
under a choice piece of the cornice

and likes it. (STAG PARTY LAUGHTER)
When are they going to show the dirty movie?

Don't cry, Miss Canada,
it's not as though the country's
in their hands.
And next year we're piping in
Congressional proceedings
direct from Washington –
    all they'll have to do
is make divorces.

INDICTMENT OF THE BLUE HOLE

        January 28 1962
You must have heard me tonight
I mentioned you 800 times
        January 28 1962
My abandoned narcotics have
abandoned me
        January 28 1962
7:30 must have dug its
pikes into your blue wrist
        January 28 1962
I shoved the transistor up my ear

And putting down
  3 loaves of suicide (?)
  2 razorblade pies
  1 De Quincey hairnet
  ~~5 gasfilled Hampstead bedsitters~~ (sic)
  a collection of oil
  ~~2 eyelash garottes~~ (sic)
  6 lysol eye foods
he said with considerable charm and travail:
Is this all I give?
One lousy reprieve
  at 2 in the morning?
This?
I'd rather have a job.

NOTHING I CAN LOSE

When I left my father's house
the sun was halfway up,
my father held it to my chin
like a buttercup.

My father was a snake oil man
a wizard, trickster, liar,
but this was his best trick,
we kissed goodbye in fire.

A mile above Niagara Falls
a dove gave me the news
of his death. I didn't miss a step,
there's nothing I can lose.

Tomorrow I'll invent a trick
I do not know tonight,
the wind, the pole will tell me what
and the friendly blinding light.

POLICE GAZETTE

My grandfather slams the silver goblet down.
He clears a silence
           in the family talk
to comment on the wine.

It's hot. Jesus is dying of heat.
There he lies on the wall
           of the sordid courtroom
trying to get air into his armpits.
Judge runs a finger
           between neck and collar –
hands the sentence down.

Love me this first day of June.
I'd rather sleep with ashes
           than priestly wisdom.
Of all the lonely places in the world
this is best
           where debris is human.
I kiss the precious ashes
that fall from fiery flesh.
On these familiar shapes
           I lay my kisses down.

Hitler is alive.
He is fourteen years old.
He does not shave.
He wants to be an architect.

The first star tonight
insanely high, virgin, calm.
I have one hour of peace
           before the documented planets
burn me down.

NO PARTNERS

dancer! cut them with your yellow hair
jawbone of silk slash them down
trouser slices lapel fragments suit debris
heaped with choppedup stumblers
beneath her grapewhite piston feet

She was hardly leaping, almost stilled by all the power in her, shoulders raised, calling in everything, her elbows pressing it into her stomach. She was a single spindle in the centre of a cobweb, gathering, growing, winding us all into particles of her supreme flesh.

She barely moved but her body screamed out motion. Her feet barely struck and lifted, almost stilled by all the power in her. Her shoulders were raised, forward, calling in everything, her elbows pressing it into her belly, fingers getting the tidbits, gathering, growing, winding us all into particles of her supreme flesh, And when we'd begone she would be in the
centre of some vast room
shimmering enormous at rest

ON THE DEATH OF AN UNCHARTED PLANET

Bilesmell in my room
Too cold to open the window
Lying on my bed
Hand over mouth
Didn't dare speak
Out of razorblades
New pimples
When suddenly
I knew it died
Clean blazing death
So bright
So irrelevant
Puff it went
Ten times the
Weight of the world
Lost to nobody
New meteors
New collisions
What comfort
At my stomach gnawed
The divine emptiness
I ate
The dirty dishes
I squeezed my face
Fat and full
Free as a bullet
I did pushups
On the 11th story
Clean blazing death
So bright
So irrelevant
Who wouldn't
Laugh himself
Into monstrous health
Just noticing it

I WANTED TO BE A DOCTOR

The famous doctor held up Grandma's stomach.
Cancer! Cancer! he cried out.
The theatre was brought low.
None of the internes thought about ambition.

Cancer! They all looked the other way.
They thought Cancer would leap out
and get them. They hated to be near.
This happened in Vilna in the Medical School.

Nobody could sit still.
They might be sitting beside Cancer.
Cancer was present.
Cancer had been let out of its bottle.

I was looking in the skylight.
I wanted to be a doctor.
All the internes ran outside.
The famous doctor held on to the stomach.

He was alone with Cancer.
Cancer! Cancer! Cancer!
He didn't care who heard or didn't hear.
It was his 87th Cancer.

ON HEARING A NAME
LONG UNSPOKEN

Listen to the stories
men tell of last year
that sound of other places
though they happened here

Listen to a name
so private it can burn
hear it said aloud
and learn and learn

History is a needle
for putting men asleep
anointed with the poison
of all they want to keep

Now a name that saved you
has a foreign taste
claims a foreign body
froze in last year's waste

And what is living lingers
while monuments are built
then yields its final whisper
to letters raised in gilt

But cries of stifled ripeness
whip me to my knees
I am with the falling snow
falling in the seas

I am with the hunters
hungry and shrewd
and I am with the hunted
quick and soft and nude

I am with the houses
that wash away in rain
and leave no teeth of pillars
to rake them up again

Let men numb names
scratch winds that blow
listen to the stories
but what you know you know

And knowing is enough
for mountains such as these
where nothing long remains
houses walls or trees

FINALLY I CALLED

Finally I called the people I didn't want to hear from
After the third ring I said
I'll let it ring five more times then what will I do
The telephone is a fine instrument
but I never learned to work it very well
Five more rings and I'll put the receiver down
I know where it goes I know that much
The telephone was black with silver rims
The booth was cozier than the drugstore
There were a lot of creams and scissors and tubes
I needed for my body
I was interested in many coughdrops
I believe the drugstore keeper hated
his telephone and people like me
who ask for change so politely
I decided to keep to the same street
and go into the fourth drugstore
and call them again

STYLE

I don't believe the radio stations
of Russia and America
but I like the music and I like
the solemn European voices announcing jazz
I don't believe opium or money
though they're hard to get
and punished with long sentences
I don't believe love
in the midst of my slavery I
do not believe
I am a man sitting in a house
on a treeless Argolic island
I will forget the grass of my mother's lawn
I know I will
I will forget the old telephone number
Fitzroy seven eight two oh
I will forget my style
I will have no style
I hear a thousand miles of hungry static
and the old clear water eating rocks
I hear the bells of mules eating
I hear the flowers eating the night
under their folds
Now a rooster with a razor
plants the haemophilia gash across
the soft black sky
and now I know for certain
I will forget my style
Perhaps a mind will open in this world
perhaps a heart will catch rain
Nothing will heal and nothing will freeze
but perhaps a heart will catch rain
America will have no style
Russia will have no style
It is happening in the twenty eighth year

of my attention
I don't know what will become
of the mules with their lady eyes
or the old clear water
or the giant rooster
The early morning greedy radio eats
the governments one by one the languages
the poppy fields one by one
Beyond the numbered band
a silence develops for every style
for the style I laboured on
an external silence like the space
between insects in a swarm
electric unremembering
and it is aimed at us
(I am sleepy and frightened)
it makes toward me brothers

GOEBBELS ABANDONS HIS NOVEL

AND JOINS THE PARTY

His last love poem
    broke in the harbour
where swearing blondes
loaded scrap
    into rusted submarines.
Out in the sun
he was surprised
    to find himself lustless
as a wheel.
More simple than money
he sat in some spilled salt

and wondered if he would find again
the scars of lampposts
ulcers of wrought iron fence.
He remembered perfectly
how he sprung
    his father's heart attack
and left his mother
in a pit
memory white from loss of guilt.
Precision in the sun
the elevators
    the pieces of iron
broke whatever thous
    his pain had left
like a whistle breaks
a gang of sweating men.
Ready to join the world
yes yes ready to marry
convinced pain a matter of choice
a Doctor of Reason
he began to count the ships
decorate the men.
Will dreams threaten
    this discipline
will favourite hair favourite thighs
last life's sweepstake winners
drive him to adventurous cafés?
Ah my darling pupils
do you think there exists a hand
so bestial in beauty so ruthless
that can switch off
his religious electric exlax light?

WHY COMMANDS ARE OBEYED

My father pulls the curtains: the Mother Goose wallpaper goes black. He insists the spaghetti is snakes and the bench a sheer cliff.

"Then why lead me, Father, if they are true snakes, if it is a sheer cliff?"

"Higher! Be brave!"

"But I was brave outside; yesterday, outside, I was very brave."

"That? That was no ordeal. This is the ordeal, this familiar room where I say the bench is dangerous."

"It's true!" I shouted twenty years later, pulling him out of his dirty bed. "Poor little Father, you told me true."

"Let me be. I am an old Father."

"No! Lift up thy nose. The window is made of axes. What is that grey matter in the ashtrays? Not from cigarettes, I'll bet. The living room is a case for relics!"

"Must I look?"

"I'll say you must. One of your young, hardly remembered legs is lodged between the pillows of the chesterfield, decaying like food between teeth. This room is a case for stinking relics!"

Yes, yes, we wept down the Turkish carpet, entangled in the great, bloodwarm, family embrace, reconciled as the old story unfolded.

It happens to everyone. For those with eyes, who know in their hearts that terror is mutual, then this hard community has a beauty of its own.

Once upon a time my father pulls the curtains: the Mother Goose wallpaper goes black it began. We heard it in each other's arms.

IT USES US!

Come upon this heap
exposed to camera leer:
would you snatch a skull
for midnight wine, my dear?

Can you wear a cape
claim these burned for you
or is this death unusable
alien and new?

In our leaders' faces
(albeit they deplore
the past) can you read how
they love Freedom more?

In my own mirror
their eyes beam at me:
my face is theirs, my eyes
burnt and free.

Now you and I are mounted
on this heap, my dear:
from this height we thrill
as boundaries disappear.

Kiss me with your teeth.

All things can be done
whisper museum ovens of
a war that Freedom won.

THE FIRST MURDER

I knew it never happened
There was no murder in the field
The grass wasn't red
The grass was green
I knew it never happened

I've come home tired
My boots are streaked with filth
What good to preach
it never happened
to the bodies murdered in the field

Tell the truth I've smoked myself
into love this innocent night
It never happened
It never happened
There was no murder in the field

There was a house on the field
The field itself was large and empty
It was night
It was dead of night
There were lights in the little windows

MY TEACHER IS DYING

Martha they say you are gentle
No doubt you labour at it
Why is it I see you
leaping into unmade beds
strangling the telephone
Why is it I see you
hiding your dirty nylons
in the fireplace
Martha talk to me
My teacher is dying
His laugh is already dead
that put cartilage
between the bony facts
Now they rattle loud
Martha talk to me
Mountain Street is dying
Apartment fifteen is dying
Apartment seven and eight are dying
All the rent is dying
Martha talk to me
I wanted all the dancers' bodies
to inhabit like his old classroom
where everything that happened
was tender and important
Martha talk to me
Toss out the fake Jap silence
Scream in my kitchen
logarithms laundry lists anything
Talk to me
My radio is falling to pieces
My betrayals are so fresh
they still come with explanations
Martha talk to me
What sordid parable
do you teach by sleeping

Talk to me
for my teacher is dying
The cars are parked
on both sides of the street
some facing north
some facing south
I draw no conclusions
Martha talk to me
I could burn my desk
when I think how perfect we are
you asleep me finishing
the last of the Saint Emilion
Talk to me gentle Martha
dreaming of percussions massacres
hair pinned to the ceiling
I'll keep your secret
Let's tell the milkman
we have decided
to marry our rooms

MONTREAL 1964

Can someone turn off the noise?
    Pearls rising on the breath of her breasts
grind like sharpening stones:
my fingernails wail as they grow their fraction
I think they want to be claws:
the bed fumes like a quicksand hole
we won't climb on it for love:
the street yearns for action nobler than traffic
red lights want to be flags
policemen want their arms frozen in loud movies:
ask a man for the time
your voice is ruined with static:
    What a racket! What strange dials!
Only Civil War can fuse it shut—
the mouth of the glorious impatient
ventriloquist performing behind our daily lives!

Canada is a dying animal
I will not be fastened to a dying animal
That's the sort of thing to say, that's good,
that will change my life.

And when my neighbour is broken for his error
and my blood guaranteed by Law against
an American failure
I dread the voice behind the flag I drew
on the blank sky
for my absolute poems will be crumpled
under a marble asylum
my absolute flight snarled like old fishing line:
What will I have in my head
to serve against logic brotherhood destiny?

WHY EXPERIENCE IS NO TEACHER

Not mine – the body you were *promised*
is buried at the heart
of an unusable machine
no one can stop or start.

You'll lie with it? You might dig deep –
escape a Law or two – see a dart
of light. You
won't get near the heart.

I tried – I am the same – come the same.
I wanted my senses to rave.
The dart was ordinary light.
Will nothing keep you here, my love, my love?

❦

FOR MY OLD LAYTON

His pain, unowned, he left
in paragraphs of love, hidden,
like a cat leaves shit
under stones, and he crept out in day,
clean, arrogant, swift, prepared
to hunt or sleep or starve.

The town saluted him with garbage
which he interpreted as praise
for his muscular grace. Orange peels,
cans, discarded guts rained like ticker-tape.
For a while he ruined their nights
by throwing his shadow in moon-full windows
as he spied on the peace of gentle folk.

Once he envied them. Now with a happy
screech he bounded from monument to monument
in their most consecrated plots, drunk
to know how close he lived to the breathless
in the ground, drunk to feel how much he loved
the snoring mates, the old, the children of the town.

Until at last, like Timon, tired
of human smell, resenting even
his own shoe-steps in the wilderness,
he chased animals, wore live snakes, weeds
for bracelets. When the sea
pulled back the tide like a blanket
he slept on stone cribs, heavy,
dreamless, the salt-bright atmosphere
like an automatic laboratory
building crystals in his hair.

THE ONLY TOURIST IN HAVANA

TURNS HIS THOUGHTS HOMEWARD

Come, my brothers,
let us govern Canada,
let us find our serious heads,
let us dump asbestos on the White House,
let us make the French talk English,
   not only here but everywhere,
let us torture the Senate individually
   until they confess,
let us purge the New Party,
let us encourage the dark races
   so they'll be lenient
   when they take over,
let us make the CBC talk English,
let us all lean in one direction
   and float down
   to the coast of Florida,
let us have tourism,
let us flirt with the enemy,
let us smelt pig-iron in our backyards,
let us sell snow
   to under-developed nations,
(Is it true one of our national leaders
   was a Roman Catholic?)
let us terrorize Alaska,
let us unite
   Church and State,
let us not take it lying down,
let us have two Governor Generals
   at the same time,
let us have another official language,
let us determine what it will be,
let us give a Canada Council Fellowship
   to the most original suggestion,
let us teach sex in the home
   to parents,

let us threaten to join the U.S.A.
    and pull out at the last moment,
my brothers, come,
our serious heads are waiting for us somewhere
    like Gladstone bags abandoned
    after a coup d'état,
let us put them on very quickly,
let us maintain a stony silence
    on the St. Lawrence Seaway.

Havana
April 1961

THE INVISIBLE TROUBLE

Too fevered to insist:
"My world is terror,"
he covers his wrist
and numbers of the war.

His arm is unburned
his flesh whole:
the numbers he learned
from a movie reel.

He covers his wrist
under the table.
The drunkards have missed
his invisible trouble.

A tune rises up.
His skin is blank!
He can't lift his cup
he can't! he can't!

The chorus grows.
So does his silence.
Nothing, he knows
there is nothing to notice.

SICK ALONE

Nursery giant hordes return
wading in the clue taste of bile
You ate too much kitchen
went green on the lone looptheloop
It will not let you off to sleep
It is too fast   It is too steep
Crash past a squashed group
of bible animals lion child kitten
Where where is your demonic smile
You vomit when you want to burn

MILLENNIUM

This could be my little
    book about love
    if I wrote it –
but my good demon said:
"Lay off documents!"
Everybody was watching me
    burn my books –
I swung my liberty torch
happy as a gestapo brute;
the only thing I wanted to save
    was a scar
    a burn or two –
    but my good demon said:
    "Lay off documents!
    The fire's not important!"
The pile was safely blazing.
I went home to take a bath.
I phoned my grandmother.
She is suffering from arthritis.
"Keep well," I said, "don't mind the pain."
    "You neither," she said.
Hours later I wondered
    did she mean
    don't mind *my* pain
    or don't mind *her* pain?
Whereupon my good demon said:
"Is that all you can do?"
        Well was it?
    Was it all I could do?
    There was the old lady
    eating alone, thinking about
      Prince Albert, Flanders Field,
    Kishenev, her fingers too sore
        for TV knobs;
    but how could I get there?

my personal fire

The books were gone
my address lists –
My good demon said again:
"Lay off documents!
   You know how to get there!"
And suddenly I did!
I remembered it from memory!
   I found her
pouring over the royal family tree,
       "Grandma,"
    I almost said,
   "you've got it upside down –"
"Take a look," she said,
"it only goes to George V."
     "That's far enough
       you sweet old blood!"
   "You're right!" she sang
       and burned the
   London Illustrated Souvenir
I did not understand
       the day it was
       till I looked outside
     and saw a fire in every
         window on the street
   and crowds of humans
       crazy to talk
and cats and dogs and birds
     smiling at each other!

animals in love   fires in every window

HITLER THE BRAIN-MOLE

Hitler the brain-mole looks out of my eyes
Goering boils ingots of gold in my bowels
My Adam's Apple bulges with the whole head of Goebbels
No use to tell a man he's a Jew
I'm making a lampshade out of your kiss
Confess! confess!
    is what you demand
although you believe you're giving me everything

DEATH OF A LEADER

Anxious to break a journey's back,
dismiss itself in ash,
the sun invaded noon:
like a bomb seen
falling from below
it widened its circumference
in the middle of the sky.

He stood on his shadow
like a dead sundial.
Children hunting a balloon
beside a monument
blended with the figures
striving on the pedestal.
Clash of gold and light
etched the Capitol dome in black.

His speeches returned,
his hours of applause,
weight of foreign medals,
white clothes of too many summers,
girls with whom he shared his power
now old and powerful.
His strategies returned
diagrammed like a geodesic sphere,
He balanced them on his forehead
weaving like a seal.

He was heavy and hot.
He'd had enough.
Let his colleagues
balance the state.
They were so distinguished
eagle-like, silver-grey.
Let him fall where his shoes were,
where his striped trousers led,
where the dove-coloured waistcoat pointed:
let him fall down in the sun.

He fell near the balloon.
Children hushed back
as if their toy
    could catch the disease.
Secret Service men,
ex-athletes chosen for their height,
made a ring around the body.
At attention they stood
while their shadows began as pools,
lengthened into spikes.
At any moment you thought
they might join hands and dance.

The city attended, still at its monuments.
Everyone was waiting.
They knew it was being prepared,
polished, painted gleaming white.
But when was it coming?
When was it coming?

The ambulance!

Havana
April 1961

ALEXANDER TROCCHI, PUBLIC

JUNKIE, PRIEZ POUR NOUS

Who is purer
　more simple than you?
Priests play poker with the burghers,
police in underwear
　leave Crime at the office,
our poets work bankers' hours
retire to wives and fame-reports.

The spike flashes in your blood
permanent as a silver lighthouse.

I'm apt to loaf
　in a coma of newspapers,
avoid the second-hand bodies
which cry to be catalogued.
I dream I'm
　a divine right Prime Minister,
I abandon plans for bloodshed in Canada.
I accept an O.B.E.

Under hard lights
with doctors' instruments
   you are at work
in the bathrooms of the city,
changing The Law.

I tend to get distracted
   by hydrogen bombs,
by Uncle's disapproval
   of my treachery
to the men's clothing industry.
I find myself
   believing public clocks,
taking advice
from the Dachau generation.

The spike hunts
constant as a compass.
   You smile like a Navajo
discovering American oil
on his official slum wilderness,
a surprise every half hour.

I'm afraid I sometimes forget
my lady's pretty little blonde package
is an amateur time-bomb
set to fizzle in my middle-age.
   I forget the Ice Cap, the pea-minds,
the heaps of expensive teeth.

You don a false nose
line up twice for the Demerol dole;
you step out of a tourist group
shoot yourself on the steps of the White House,
you try to shoot the big arms
   of the Lincoln Memorial;
through a flaw in their lead houses
you spy on scientists,
   stumble on a cure for scabies;
you drop pamphlets from a stolen jet:

"The Truth about Junk";
you pirate a national tv commercial
shove your face against
   the window of the living-room
insist that healthy skin is grey.

A little blood in the sink
Red cog-wheels
   shaken from your arm
punctures inflamed
like a roadmap showing cities
over 10,000 pop.

Your arms tell me
you have been reaching into the coke machine
for strawberries,
you have been humping the thorny crucifix
you have been piloting Mickey Mouse balloons
through the briar patch,
you have been digging for grins in the tooth-pile.

Bonnie Queen Alex Eludes Montreal Hounds
Famous Local Love Scribe Implicated

Your purity drives me to work.
I must get back to lust and microscopes,
experiments in enbalming,
resume the census of my address book.

You leave behind you a fanatic
to answer RCMP questions.

THREE GOODNIGHTS

Out of some simple part of me
which I cannot use up
    I took a blessing for the flowers
tightening in the night
like fists of jealous love
    like knots
no one can undo without destroying
    The new morning gathered me
in blue mist
    like dust under a wedding gown
Then I followed the day
like a cloud of heavy sheep
    after the judas
up a blood-ringed ramp
into the terror of every black building

Ten years sealed journeys unearned dreams
Laughter meant to tempt me into old age
    spilled for friends stars unknown flesh mules Sea
Instant knowledge of bodies material and spirit
    which slowly learned would have made death smile
Stories turning into theories
    which begged only for the telling and retelling
Girls sailing over the blooms of my mouth
    with a muscular triangular kiss
    ordinary mouth to secret mouth
Nevertheless my homage sticky flowers
    rabbis green and red serving the sun like platters
In the end you offered me the dogma you taught
    me to disdain and I good pupil disdained it
I fell under the diagrammed fields like the fragment
    of a perfect statue layers of cities build upon
I saw you powerful I saw you happy
    that I could not live only for harvesting
that I was a true citizen of the slow earth

Light and Splendour
in the sleeping orchards
entering the trees
like a silent movie wedding procession
entering the arches of branches
for the sake of love only
From a hill I watched
the apple blossoms breathe
the silver out of the night
like fish eating the spheres
of air out of the river
So the illumined night fed
the sleeping orchards
entering the vaults of branches
like a holy procession
Long live the Power of Eyes
Long live the invisible steps
men can read on a mountain
Long live the unknown machine
or heart
which by will or accident
pours with victor's grace
endlessly perfect weather
on the perfect creatures
the world grows

Montreal
July 1964

TO A MAN WHO THINKS

HE IS MAKING AN ANGEL

Drop the angel out of your silver spoon
You'll never get it to your mouth
You're not dealing with the moon anymore
or corkscrew unicorns

The moon you kept in a cup
herds of magic beasts in your pocket
but this real angel knocks down factories
with a wisp of hair

Do you think your arms are wide enough
to cramp her in your heritage
you with your iron maidens
brimstone ponds where only sufferers sing

Do you think she's from Chartres you turd
From Notre Dame out of any church you know
or even out of some humble inflamed mystic's mind
She is from a service you have never heard

Ah but she stops my mouth from further curses
covering my whole heaving body with one of her molecules

ON THE SICKNESS OF MY LOVE

Poems!   break out!
break my head!
What good's a skull?
Help!   help!
I need you!

She is getting old.
Her body tells her everything.
She has put aside cosmetics.
She is a prison of truth.

Make her get up!
dance the seven veils!
Poems!   silence her body!
Make her friend of mirrors!

Do I have to put on my cape?
wander like the moon
over skies & skies of flesh
to depart again in the morning?

Can't I pretend
she grows prettier?
be a convict?
Can't my power fool me?
Can't I live in poems?

Hurry up!   poems!   lies!
Damn your weak music!
You've let arthritis in!
You're no poem
you're a visa.

CRUEL BABY

Where did you learn mouthfuls for everything,
O Dweller in Childsmelling Cloakrooms?

Chief, do I have to come down and identify
the bodies I loved?

I forget, I said I forget which breast it was.
Hers?   Yes.   Good.   Ask her many questions,
find out, do her horoscope.

Hooray!   she has a family name.
Hooray!   she looks like her grandmother.

Doctor Reich call surgery:
show anal slides of blue come.

Cruel Baby, you lost the world:
you ate dictionaries of flowers:
you fell for particular beauty.

FOR MARIANNE

It's so simple
to wake up beside your ears
and count the pearls
with my two heads

It takes me back to blackboards
and I'm running with Jane
and seeing the dog run

It makes it so easy
to govern this country
I've already thought up the laws
I'll work hard all day
in Parliament

Then let's go to bed
right after supper
Let's sleep and wake up
all night

THE FAILURE OF A SECULAR LIFE

The pain-monger came home
from a hard day's torture.

He came home with his tongs.
He put down his black bag.

His wife hit him with an open nerve
and a cry the trade never heard.

He watched her real-life Dachau,
knew his career was ruined.

Was there anything else to do?
He sold his bag and tongs,

went to pieces. A man's got to be able
to bring his wife something.

MY MENTORS

My rabbi has a silver buddha,
my priest has a jade talisman.
My doctor sees a marvellous omen
in our prolonged Indian summer.

My rabbi, my priest stole their trinkets
from shelves in the holy of holies.
The trinkets cannot be eaten.
They wonder what to do with them.

My doctor is happy as a pig
although he is dying of exposure.
He has finished his big book
on the phallus as a phallic symbol.

My zen master is a grand old fool.
I caught him worshipping me yesterday,
so I made him stand in a foul corner
with my rabbi, my priest, and my doctor.

HYDRA 1960

Anything that moves is white,
a gull, a wave, a sail,
and moves too purely to be aped.
Smash the pain.

Never pretend peace.
The consolumentum has not,
never will be kissed. Pain
cannot compromise this light.

Do violence to the pain,
ruin the easy vision,
the easy warning, water
for those who need to burn.

These are ruthless: rooster shriek,
bleached goat skull.
Scalpels grow with poppies
if you see them truly red.

LEVIATHAN

I learn nothing
because my mind is stuffed with bodies:
blurred parades, hosts of soft lead wings,
tragic heaped holes of the starved,
    the tangled closer than snakes,
swarming gymnasiums,
refuse of hospitals compose my mind:
no neat cells,
limbs, rumps, fetuses compose my mind.

It reels like Leviathan in oldtime cuts,
a nation writhing:
mothers, statues, madonnas, ruins –
I'm stripped, suckled, weaned,
I leap, love, anonymous as insect.
There is no beauty to choose here:
    some mutilated, some whole, some perfect severed thighs,
embryos, dried skin:
the mass so vast some scales, some liquid never meeting.

Language is gone,
squeezed out in food, kisses.
Arithmetic, power, cities never were.
God knows what they've built today.
    Only the echo I cast in world offices
returns to damn me ignorant –
as if I can hear in the screech of flesh
or talk back with mouth of hair.

HEIRLOOM

The torture scene developed under a glass bell
such as might protect an expensive clock.
I almost expected a chime to sound
as the tongs were applied
and the body jerked and fainted calm.
All the people were tiny and rosy-cheeked
and if I could have heard a cry of triumph or pain
it would have been tiny as the mouth that made it
or one single note of a music box.
The drama bell was mounted

like a gigantic baroque pearl
on a wedding ring or brooch or locket.
   I know you feel naked, little darling.
I know you hate living in the country
and can't wait until the shiny magazines
come every week and every month.
Look through your grandmother's house again.
There is an heirloom somewhere.

PROMISE

Your blond hair
is the way I live –
smashed by light!

Your mouth-print
is the birthmark
on my power.

To love you
is to live
my ideal diary

which I have
promised my body
I will never write!

SKY

The great ones pass
they pass without touching
they pass without looking
each in his joy
each in his fire
Of one another
they have no need
they have the deepest need
The great ones pass

Recorded in some multiple sky
inlaid in some endless laughter
they pass
like stars of different seasons
like meteors of different centuries

Fire undiminished
by passing fire
laughter uncorroded
by comfort
they pass one another
without touching without looking
needing only to know
the great ones pass

WAITING FOR MARIANNE

I have lost a telephone
with your smell in it

I am living beside the radio
all the stations at once
but I pick out a Polish lullaby
I pick it out of the static
it fades I wait I keep the beat
it comes back almost asleep

Did you take the telephone
knowing I'd sniff it immoderately
maybe heat up the plastic
to get all the crumbs of your breath

and if you won't come back
how will you phone to say
you won't come back
so that I could at least argue

WHY I HAPPEN TO BE FREE

They all conspire to make me free
I tried to join their arguments
but there were so few sides
and I needed several

          Forsaking the lovely girl
was not my idea
but she fell asleep in somebody's bed
          Now more than ever
I want enemies
          You who thrive
in the easy world of modern love
look out for me
for I have developed a terrible virginity
and meeting me
all who have done more than kiss
will perish in shame
with warts and hair on their palms
          Time was our best men died
in error and enlightenment
Moses on the lookout
David in his house of blood
Camus beside the driver
          My new laws encourage
not satori but perfection
at last at last
          Jews who walk
too far on Sabbath
will be stoned
          Catholics who blaspheme
electricity applied
to their genitals
          Buddhists who acquire property
sawn in half
          Naughty Protestants
have governments
to make them miserable
          Ah the universe returns to order
The new Montreal skyscrapers
bully the parking lots
like the winners of a hygiene contest
          a suite of windows lit here and there
like a First Class ribbon
for extra cleanliness
          A girl I knew
sleeps in some bed

and of all the lovely things
I might say I say this
        I see her body puzzled
with the mouthprints
of all the kisses of all the men
she's known
        like a honky-tonk piano
ringed with years of cocktail glasses
and while she cranks and tinkles
in the quaint old sinful dance
        I walk through
the blond November rain
punishing her with my happiness

THE TRUE DESIRE

The food that will not obey. It longs for its old shape. The grapes dream of the tight cluster, resume their solidarity. The meat, in some rebellious collusion with the stomach, unchews itself, unites into the original butcher's slab, red, defiant, recalling even the meadow life of the distant dead animal. But perhaps the stomach is guiltless, for here is cheese, mauled and in disarray, but refusing absolutely to interact with gastric juices. The food has no hope of real life, but still, in these regained, however mutilated shapes, it resists, and for its victories claims the next day's hunger and the body's joy.

There is a whitewashed hotel waiting for me somewhere, in which I will begin my fast and my new life.

Oh to stand in the Ganges wielding a yard of intestine.

THE WAY BACK

But I am not lost
any more than leaves are lost
or buried vases
This is not my time
I would only give you second thoughts

I know you must call me traitor
because I have wasted my blood
in aimless love
and you are right
Blood like that
never won an inch of star

You know how to call me
although such a noise now
would only confuse the air
Neither of us can forget
the steps we danced
the words you stretched
to call me out of dust

Yes I long for you
not just as a leaf for weather
or vase for hands
but with a narrow human longing
that makes a man refuse
any fields but his own

I wait for you at an
unexpected place in your journey
like the rusted key
or the feather you do not pick up
until the way back
after it is clear
the remote and painful destination
changed nothing in your life

THE PROJECT

Evidently they need a lot of blood for these tests. I let them take all they wanted. The hospital was cool and its atmosphere of order encouraged me to persist in my own projects.

I always wanted to set fire to your houses. I've been in them. Through the front doors and the back. I'd like to see them burn slowly so I could visit many and peek in the falling windows. I'd like to see what happens to those white carpets you pretended to be so careless about. I'd like to see a white telephone melting.

We don't want to trap too many inside because the streets have got to be packed with your poor bodies screaming back and forth. I'll be comforting. Oh dear, pyjama flannel seared right on to the flesh. Let me pull it off.

It seems to me they took too much blood. Probably selling it on the side. The little man's white frock was smeared with blood. Little men like that keep company with blood. See them in abatoirs and assisting in human experiments.

– When did you last expose yourself?
– Sunday morning for a big crowd in the lobby of the Queen Elizabeth.
– Funny. You know what I mean.
– Expose myself to what?
– A woman.
– Ah.

I narrowed my eyes and whispered in his yellow ear.
– You better bring her in too.
– And it's still free?

Of course it was still free. Not counting the extra blood they stole. Prevent my disease from capturing the entire city. Help this man. Give him all possible Judeo-Christian help.

Fire would be best. I admit that. Tie firebrands between the foxes and chase them through your little gardens. A rosy sky would improve the view from anywhere. It would be a mercy. Oh, to see the roofs devoured and the beautiful old level of land rising again.

The factory where I work isn't far from the hospital. Same architect as a matter of fact and the similarities don't end there. It's easier to get away with lying down in the hospital. However we have our comforts in the factory.

The foreman winked at me when I went back to my machine. He loved his abundant nature. Me new at the job and he'd actually given me time off. I really enjoy the generosity of slaves. He came over to inspect my work.

– But this won't do at all.
– No?
– The union said you were an experienced operator.
– I am. I am.
– This is no seam.
– Now that you mention it.
– Look here.

He took a fresh trouser and pushed in beside me on the bench. He was anxious to demonstrate the only skill he owned. He arranged the pieces under the needle. When he was halfway down the leg and doing very nicely I brought my foot down on the pedal beside his. The unexpected acceleration sucked his fingers under the needle.

Another comfort is the Stock Room.

It is large and dark and filled with bundles and rolls of material.

– But shouldn't you be working?
– No, Mary, I shouldn't.
– Won't Sam miss you?
– You see he's in the hospital. Accident.

Mary runs the Cafeteria and the Boss exposes himself to her regularly. This guarantees her the concession.

I feel the disease raging in my blood. I expect my saliva to be discoloured.

– Yes, Mary, real cashmere. Three hundred dollar suits.

The Boss has a wife to whom he must expose himself every once in a while. She has her milkmen. The city is orderly. There are white bottles standing in front of a million doors. And there are Conventions. Multitudes of bosses sharing the pleasures of exposure.

I shall go mad. They'll find me at the top of Mount Royal impersonating Genghis Khan. Seized with laughter and pus.

– Very soft, Mary. That's what they pay for.

Fire would be best. Flames. Bright windows. Two cars exploding in each garage. But could I ever manage it. This way is slower. More heroic in a way. Less dramatic of course. But I have an imagination.

HYDRA 1963

The stony path coiled around me
and bound me to the night.
A boat hunted the edge of the sea
under a hissing light.

Something soft involved a net
and bled around a spear.
The blunt death, the cumulus jet —
I spoke to you, I thought you near!

Or was the night so black
that something died alone?
A man with a glistening back
beat the food against a stone.

ALL THERE IS TO KNOW
ABOUT ADOLPH EICHMANN

EYES: .... Medium
HAIR: .... Medium
WEIGHT: .... Medium
HEIGHT: .... Medium
DISTINGUISHING FEATURES: .... None
NUMBER OF FINGERS: .... Ten
NUMBER OF TOES: .... Ten
INTELLIGENCE: .... Medium

What did you expect?

Talons?

Oversize incisors?

Green saliva?

Madness?

THE NEW LEADER

When he learned that his father had the oven contract, that the smoke above the city, the clouds as warm as skin, were his father's manufacture, he was freed from love, his emptiness was legalized.

Hygienic as a whip his heart drove out the alibis of devotion, free as a storm-severed bridge, useless and pure as drowned alarm clocks, he breathed deeply, gratefully in the polluted atmosphere, and he announced : My father had the oven contract, he loved my mother and built her houses in the countryside.

When he learned his father had the oven contract he climbed a hillock of eyeglasses, he stood on a drift of hair, he hated with great abandon the king cripples and their mothers, the husbands and wives, the familiar sleep, the decent burdens.

Dancing down Ste Catherine Street he performed great surgery on a hotel of sleepers. The windows leaked like a broken meat freezer. His hatred blazed white on the salted driveways. He missed nobody but he was happy he'd taken one hunded and fifty women in moonlight back in ancient history.

He was drunk at last, drunk at last, after years of threading history's crushing daisy-chain with beauty after beauty. His father had raised the thigh-shaped clouds which smelled of salesmen, gypsies and violinists. With the certainty and genital pleasure of revelation he knew, he could not doubt, his father was the one who had the oven contract.

Drunk at last, he hugged himself, his stomach clean, cold and drunk, the sky clean but only for him, free to shiver, free to hate, free to begin.

HOW IT HAPPENED IN THE

MIDDLE OF THE DAY

Hate jumped out of the way.
Sorrow left with a squashed somersault
like a cripple winning candy from rich ladies.
Angels of reason and joy
plus other Apollonian yes-men at home
on account of sunstroke
contributed their absence to the miracle.
The demons of adulterers, everyday drunks,
professional irrationalists, the fatuous possessed,
these cheap easy demons so common
to the courting procedure,
refused to appear due to insufficient publicity.
No shark put its fin on the lips
of the little waves
like a schoolmistress demanding silence
lest drama threaten the miracle.
Someone began over again and failed –
noting not a single alien tremor
in the voices crying: tomatoes, onions, bread.

FOR E.J.P.

I once believed a single line
    in a Chinese poem could change
        forever how blossoms fell
and that the moon itself climbed on
    the grief of concise weeping men
        to journey over cups of wine
I thought invasions were begun for crows
    to pick at a skeleton
        dynasties sown and spent
to serve the language of a fine lament
    I thought governors ended their lives
        as sweetly drunken monks
telling time by rain and candles
    instructed by an insect's pilgrimage
        across the page – all this
so one might send an exile's perfect letter
to an ancient hometown friend

I chose a lonely country
    broke from love
        scorned the fraternity of war
I polished my tongue against the pumice moon
    floated my soul in cherry wine
        a perfumed barge for Lords of Memory
to languish on to drink to whisper out
    their store of strength
        as if beyond the mist along the shore
their girls their power still obeyed
    like clocks wound for a thousand years
I waited until my tongue was sore

Brown petals wind like fire around my poems
    I aimed them at the stars but
        like rainbows they were bent
before they sawed the world in half

Who can trace the canyoned paths
cattle have carved out of time
wandering from meadowlands to feasts
Layer after layer of autumn leaves
are swept away
Something forgets us perfectly

THE GLASS DOG

*Let me renew myself
in the midst of all the things of the world
which cannot be connected.*

The sky is empty at last,
the stars stand for themselves,
heroes and their history passed
like talk on the wind, like bells.

Flowers do not stand for love,
or if they do – not mine.
The white happens beside the mauve.
I have no laws to bind

their hunger to my own.
The same, the same, the doctors say,
for they find themselves alone:
the bread of law is dry.

I walked over the mountain with my glass dog.
The mushrooms trembled and balls of rain
fell off their roofs.
I whistled at the trees to come closer:
they jumped at the chance:
apples, acorns popped through the air.
Dandelions by the million
staggered into parachutes. A white jewelled
wind in the shape of an immense spool of gauze
swaddled every moving limb.
I collapsed slowly over the water-filled pebbles.

*

"Lambs in bags are borne by mules.
 Rough bags bruise live necks,
 three in a bag.
 It only hurts when they laugh.

"They'll hang with chickens, head down,
 white chicks in blood shops,
 block shops, cut shops.
 It only hurts when they bleed.

"Boats named for George and Barbara,
 sterns faded rose and blue,
 do their simple business
 in the bottle of the sea.

"Thalassa, thalassa, in the blackest
 weather still you keep somewhere
 among your million mirrors
 the fact of the highest gull.

"Mules flirt with brother slave brick boats."
 Give the man who said all that
 an evil shiny eggplant.
 Give him a mucous-hued octopus.

Glory bells, boys in the towers
flying the huge bells like kites,
tear the vespers out of the stoned heart.
A man has betrayed everything!

Creature! Come! One more chance. The Sea of Tin Cans. The Sea of Ruined Laboratory Eyes. The Sea of Luminous Swimmers. The Sea of Rich Tackle. The Sea of Garbage Flowers. The Sea of Sun Limbs. The Sea of Blood Jellyfish. The Sea of Dynamite. Our Lady of the Miraculous Tin Ikon. Our Blue Lady of Boats. Our Beloved Lady of Holiday Flags. Our Supreme Girl of Enduring Feathers. Bang Bang bells Bang in iron simple blue.

A MIGRATING DIALOGUE

He was wearing a black moustache and leather hair.
We talked about the gypsies.

Don't bite your nails, I told him.
Don't eat carpets.
Be careful of the rabbits.
Be cute.
Don't stay up all night watching
parades on the Very Very Very Late Show.
Don't ka-ka in your uniform.

And what about all the good generals,
the fine old aristocratic fighting men,
the brave Junkers, the brave Rommels,
the brave von Silverhaired Ambassadors
who resigned in 41?

Wipe that smirk off your face.
Captain Marvel signed the whip contract.
Joe Palooka manufactured whips.
Li'l Abner packed the whips in cases.
The Katzenjammer Kids thought up experiments.
Mere cogs.

Peekaboo Miss Human Soap.
It never happened.
O castles on the Rhine.
O blond SS.
Don't believe everything you see in museums.

I said WIPE THAT SMIRK including
the mouth-foam of superior disgust.
I don't like the way you go to work every morning.
How come the buses still run?
How come they're still making movies?

I believe with a perfect faith in the Second World War.
I am convinced that it happened.
I am not so sure about the First World War.
The Spanish Civil War – maybe.
I believe in gold teeth.
I believe in Churchill.
Don't tell me we dropped fire into cribs.
I think you are exaggerating.
The Treaty of Westphalia has faded like a lipstick
smudge on the Blarney Stone.
Napoleon was a sexy brute.
Hiroshima was Made in Japan out of paper.
I think we should let sleeping ashes lie.
I believe with a perfect faith in all the history
I remember, but it's getting harder and harder
to remember much history.

There is sad confetti sprinkling
from the windows of departing trains.
I let them go. I cannot remember them.
They hoot mournfully out of my daily life.
I forget the big numbers,
I forget what they mean.
I apologize to the special photogravure section
of a 1945 newspaper which began my education.
I apologize left and right.
I apologize in advance to all the folks
in this fine wide audience for my tasteless closing remarks.

Braun, Raubal and him
(I have some experience in these matters),
these three humans,
I can't get their nude and loving bodies out of my mind.

THE BUS

I was the last passenger of the day,
I was alone on the bus,
I was glad they were spending all that money
just getting me up Eighth Avenue.
Driver! I shouted, it's you and me tonight,
let's run away from this big city
to a smaller city more suitable to the heart,
let's drive past the swimming pools of Miami Beach,
you in the driver's seat, me several seats back,
but in the racial cities we'll change places
so as to show how well you've done up North,
and let us find ourselves some tiny American fishing village
in unknown Florida
and park right at the edge of the sand,
a huge bus pointing out,
metallic, painted, solitary,
with New York plates.

LAUNDRY

I took a backward look
As I walked down the street
My wife was hanging laundry
Sheet after sheet after sheet

She ran them down the clothesline
Like flags above a ship
Her mouth was full of clothespins
They twisted up her lip

At last I saw her ugly
Now I could not stay
I made an X across her face
But a sheet got in the way

Then the wind bent back
This flag of armistice
I made the X again
As a child repeats a wish

The second X I drew
Set me up in trade
I will never find the faces
For all goodbyes I've made

THE REST IS DROSS

We meet at a hotel
with many quarters for the radio
surprised that we've survived as lovers
not each other's
but lovers still
with outrageous hope and habits in the craft
which embarrass us slightly
as we let them be known
the special caress the perfect inflammatory word
the starvation we do not tell about
We do what only lovers can
    make a gift out of necessity
Looking at our clothes
folded over the chair
I see we no longer follow fashion
and we own our own skins
God I'm happy we've forgotten nothing
and can love each other
for years in the world

HOW THE WINTER GETS IN

I ask you where you want to go
you say nowhere
    but your eyes make a wish
An absent chiropractor
you stroke my wrist
    I'm almost fooled into
greasy circular snores
when I notice your eyes
    sounding the wall for
dynamite points
like a doctor at work on a TB chest
    Nowhere you say again in a kiss
go to sleep
First tell me your wish
    Your lashes startle on my skin
like a seismograph
An airliner's perishing drone
    pulls the wall off our room
like an old band-aid
The winter comes in
    and the eyes I don't keep
tie themselves to a journey
like wedding tin cans

Ways Mills
November 1963

PROPAGANDA

The coherent statement was made
by father, the gent with spats to
keep his shoes secret. It had to
do with the nature of religion and
the progress of lust in the twentieth
century. I myself have several
statements of a competitive
coherence which I intend to spread
around at no little expense. I
love the eternal moment, for
instance. My father used to remark,
doffing his miniature medals, that
there is a time that is ripe for
everything. A little extravagant,
Dad, I guess, judging by values.
Oh well, he'd say, and the whole
world might have been the address.

OPIUM AND HITLER

Several faiths
bid him leap –
opium and Hitler
let him sleep.

A Negress with
an appetite
helped him think
he wasn't white.

Opium and Hitler
made him sure
the world was glass.
There was no cure

for matter
disarmed as this:
the state rose on
a festered kiss.

Once a dream
nailed on the sky
a summer sun
while it was high.

He wanted a
blindfold of skin,
he wanted the
afternoon to begin.

One law broken –
nothing held.
The world was wax,
his to mould.

No! He fumbled
for his history dose.
The sun came loose,
his woman close.

Lost in a darkness
their bodies would reach,
the Leader started
a racial speech.

FOR ANYONE DRESSED IN MARBLE

The miracle we all are waiting for
is waiting till the Parthenon falls down
and House of Birthdays is a house no more
and fathers are unpoisoned by renown.
The medals and the records of abuse
can't help us on our pilgrimage to lust,
but like whips certain perverts never use,
compel our flesh in paralysing trust.
    I see an orphan, lawless and serene,
standing in a corner of the sky,
body something like bodies that have been,
but not the scar of naming in his eye.
Bred close to the ovens, he's burnt inside.
Light, wind, cold, dark – they use him like a bride.

WHEELS, FIRECLOUDS

I shot my eyes through the drawers of your empty coffins,
I was loyal,
I was one who lifted up his face.

FOLK

    flowers for hitler the summer yawned
    flowers all over my new grass
    and here is a little village
    they are painting it for a holiday
    here is a little church
    here is a school
    here are some doggies making love
    the flags are bright as laundry
    flowers for hitler the summer yawned

I HAD IT FOR A MOMENT

I had it for a moment
I knew why I must thank you
    I saw powerful governing men in black suits
I saw them undressed
in the arms of young mistresses
the men more naked than the naked women
the men crying quietly
    No that is not it
I'm losing why I must thank you
which means I'm left with pure longing
    How old are you
Do you like your thighs
I had it for a moment

I had a reason for letting the picture
of your mouth destroy my conversation
    Something on the radio
the end of a Mexican song
I saw the musicians getting paid
they are not even surprised
they knew it was only a job
    Now I've lost it completely
A lot of people think you are beautiful
How do I feel about that
I have no feeling about that
    I had a wonderful reason for not merely
courting you
It was tied up with the newspapers
    I saw secret arrangements in high offices
I saw men who loved their worldliness
even though they had looked through
big electric telescopes
they still thought their worldliness was serious
not just a hobby a taste a harmless affectation
    they thought the cosmos listened
I was suddenly fearful
one of their obscure regulations
could separate us
    I was ready to beg for mercy
Now I'm getting into humiliation
I've lost why I began this
I wanted to talk about your eyes
I know nothing about your eyes
and you've noticed how little I know
I want you somewhere safe
far from high offices
    I'll study you later
So many people want to cry quietly beside you

July 4, 1963

ISLAND BULLETIN

Oh can my fresh white trousers
and the gardenia forest
and The Rise and Fall of the Third Reich
and my heroic tan
and my remarkable quaint house
and my Italian sun-glasses
   can they do for me
what our first meeting did?
I am so good with fire yet I hesitate
to begin again
believing perhaps in some ordeal by property
I am standing by the Sunset Wall
proud
thin despite my luxury
In my journey I know I am
somewhere beyond the travelling pack of poets
I am a man of tradition
I will remain here until
I am sure what I am leaving

July 4, 1963

INDEPENDENCE

Tonight I will live with my new white skin
which I found under a millennium of pith clothing
None of the walls jump when I call them
Trees smirked *you're one of us now*
when I strode through the wheat in my polished boots
Out of control awake and newly naked
I lie back in the luxury of my colour
Somebody is marching for me at me to me
Somebody has a flag I did not invent
I think the Aztecs have not been sleeping
Magic moves from hand to hand like money
I thought we were the bank the end of the line
New York City was just a counter
the crumpled bill passed across
I thought that heroes meant us
I have been reading too much history
and writing too many history books
Magic moves from hand to hand and I'm broke
Someone stops the sleepwalker in the middle of the opera
and pries open his fist finger by finger
and kisses him goodbye
I think the Aztecs have not been sleeping
no matter what I taught the children
I think no one has ever slept but he
who gathers the past into stories
Magic moves from hand to hand
Somebody is smiling in one of our costumes
Somebody is stepping out of a costume
I think that is what invisible means

July 4, 1963

THE HOUSE

Two hours off the branch and burnt
the petals of the gardenia curl and deepen
in the yellow-brown of waste
    Your body wandered close
    I didn't raise my hand to reach
the distance was so familiar
Our house is happy with its old furniture
the black Venetian bed stands on gold claws
guarding the window
    Don't take the window away
    and leave a hole in the stark mountains
The clothesline and the grey clothespins
would make you think we're going to be together always
    Last night I dreamed
    you were Buddha's wife
and I was a historian watching you sleep
What vanity
    A girl told me something beautiful
    Very early in the morning
she saw an orange-painted wooden boat
come into port over the smooth sea
The cargo was hay
The boat rode low under the weight
She couldn't see the sailors
but on top of all the hay sat a monk
Because of the sun behind he seemed
to be sitting in a fire
like that famous photograph
    I forgot to tell you the story
    She surprised me by telling it
and I wanted her for ten minutes
I really enjoyed the gardenia from Sophia's courtyard
You put it on my table two hours ago
    and I can smell it everywhere in the house
Darling I attach nothing to it

July 4, 1963

ORDER

In many movies I came upon an idol
I would not touch, whose forehead jewel
was safe, or if stolen – mourned.
Truly, I wanted the lost forbidden city
to be the labyrinth for wise technicolor
birds, and every human riddle
the love-fed champion pursued
I knew was bad disguise for greed.
I was with the snake who made his nest
in the voluptuous treasure, I dropped
with the spider to threaten the trail-bruised
white skin of the girl who was searching
for her brother, I balanced on the limb
with the leopard who had to be content
with Negroes and double-crossers
and never tasted but a slash of hero flesh.
Even after double-pay I deserted
with the bearers, believing every rumour
the wind brought from the mountain pass.
The old sorceress, the spilled wine,
the black cards convinced me :
the timeless laws must not be broken.
When the lovers got away with the loot
of new-valued life or love, or bought
themselves a share in time by letting
the avalanche seal away for ever
the gold goblets and platters, I knew
a million ways the jungle might have been
meaner and smarter. As the red sun
came down on their embrace I shouted
from my velvet seat, Get them, get them,
to all the animals drugged with anarchy and happiness.

August 6, 1963

DESTINY

I want your warm body to disappear
politely and leave me alone in the bath
because I want to consider my destiny.
Destiny! why do you find me in this bathtub,
idle, alone, unwashed, without even
the intention of washing except at the last moment?
Why don't you find me at the top of a telephone pole,
repairing the lines from city to city?
Why don't you find me riding a horse through Cuba,
a giant of a man with a red machete?
Why don't you find me explaining machines
to underprivileged pupils, negroid Spaniards,
happy it is not a course in creative writing?
Come back here, little warm body,
it's time for another day.
Destiny has fled and I settle for you
who found me staring at you in a store
one afternoon four years ago
and slept with me every night since.
How do you find my sailor eyes after all this time?
Am I what you expected?
Are we together too much?
Did Destiny shy at the double Turkish towel,
our knowledge of each other's skin,
our love which is a proverb on the block,
our agreement that in matters spiritual
I should be the Man of Destiny
and you should be the Woman of the House?

QUEEN VICTORIA AND ME

Queen Victoria
my father and all his tobacco loved you
I love you too in all your forms
the slim unlovely virgin anyone would lay
the white figure floating among German beards
the mean governess of the huge pink maps
the solitary mourner of a prince
Queen Victoria
I am cold and rainy
I am dirty as a glass roof in a train station
I feel like an empty cast-iron exhibition
I want ornaments on everything
because my love she gone with other boys
Queen Victoria
do you have a punishment under the white lace
will you be short with her
and make her read little Bibles
will you spank her with a mechanical corset
I want her pure as power
I want her skin slightly musty with petticoats
will you wash the easy bidets out of her head
Queen Victoria
I'm not much nourished by modern love
Will you come into my life
with your sorrow and your black carriages
and your perfect memory
Queen Victoria
The 20th century belongs to you and me
Let us be two severe giants
(not less lonely for our partnership)
who discolour test tubes in the halls of science
who turn up unwelcome at every World's Fair
heavy with proverb and correction
confusing the star-dazed tourists
with our incomparable sense of loss

THE PURE LIST AND

THE COMMENTARY

The Pure List

The alarm clock invented the day
Savana the evil scientist
I loved you in blouses
It's the laundry ringing
Your bra was so flimsy
Albert Hotel sixth floor
A shoe box of drugs
I looked for you in the audience
Lie down forever in the Photomat
Your sister has blond hair
Does Perception work
Do you say zero or oh
Very few people have thighs

Etc.

The Commentary

1. The alarm clock invented the day. Luckily the glass was broken and I could twist the black moustaches. They turned into angry black whips tethered to a screw in the middle of a sundial, writhing to get free.
2. Savana the evil scientist, foe of Captain Marvel and the entire Marvel family, I summon you from your migrating Mosaic grave. Tireless worker! If I must lose, let me lose like thee!
3. I loved you in blouses. I rubbed sun-tan lotion on your back and other parts. I did this in all seasons. I loved you in old-fashioned garters. I wanted to make a brown photograph about you and pass it around cloakrooms. I would have snatched it away from someone and beat up his face.
4. It's the laundry ringing, ringing, ringing. It's a lovely sound for a Saturday morning, n'est-ce pas? The delivery boy has no place else to go. He is of a different race. Perhaps he's looked through my shirts. I think these people know too much about us.
5. Your bra was so flimsy and light, just a tantalizing formality. I thought it would die in my pocket like a corsage.
6. Albert Hotel sixth floor seven thirty p.m. On the scratched table I set out in a row a copper bust of Stalin, a plaster of paris bust of Beethoven, a china jug shaped like Winston Churchill's head, a reproduction of a fragment of the True Cross, a small idol, a photograph of a drawing of the Indian Chief Pontiac, hair, an applicator used for artificial insemination. I undressed and waited for power.
7. A shoe box of drugs. Isn't this carrying deception too far? Where will you keep your shoes?
8. I looked for you in the audience when I delivered the Memorial Lecture. Ladies and Gents, the honour is the same but the pleasure is somewhat diminished. I had expected, I had hoped to find among your faces a face which once – No, I have said too much. Let me continue. The pith of plant stems, the marrow of bones, the cellular, central, inner part of animal hair, the medulla oblongata . . . I exposed these fine minds to bravery, Etc.

THE NEW STEP

A Ballet-Drama in One Act

CHARACTERS:
MARY and DIANE, two working girls who room together. MARY is very plain, plump, clumsy: ugly, if one is inclined to the word. She is the typical victim of beauty courses and glamour magazines. Her life is a search for, a belief in the technique, the elixir, the method, the secret, the hint that will transform and render her forever lovely. DIANE is a natural beauty, tall, fresh and graceful, one of the blessed. She moves to a kind of innocent sexual music, incapable of any gesture which could intrude on this high animal grace. To watch her pull on her nylons is all one needs of ballet or art.

HARRY is the man Diane loves. He has the proportions we associate with Greek statuary. Clean, tall, openly handsome, athletic. He glitters with health, decency, and mindlessness.

THE COLLECTOR is a woman over thirty, grotesquely obese, a great heap, deformed, barely mobile. She possesses a commanding will and combines the fascination of the tyrant and the freak. Her jolliness asks for no charity. All her movements represent the triumph of a rather sinister spiritual energy over an intolerable mass of flesh.

SCENE:
It is eight o'clock of a Saturday night. All the action takes place in the girls' small apartment which need be furnished with no more than a dressing-mirror, wardrobe, record-player, easy chair, and a front door. We have the impression, as we do from the dwelling places of most bachelor girls, of an arrangement they want to keep comfortable but temporary.

DIANE is dressed in bra and panties, preparing herself for an evening with HARRY. MARY follows her about the room, lost in envy and awe, handing DIANE the necessary lipstick or brush, doing up a button or fastening a necklace. MARY is the dull but orthodox assistant to DIANE's mysterious ritual of beauty.

MARY: What is it like?
DIANE: What like?
MARY: You know.
DIANE: No.
MARY: To be like you.
DIANE: Such as?
MARY: Beautiful.
(*Pause. During these pauses* DIANE *continues her toilet as does* MARY *her attendance.*)
DIANE: Everybody can be beautiful.
MARY: You can say that.
DIANE: Love makes people beautiful.
MARY: You can say that.
DIANE: A woman in love is beautiful.
(*Pause.*)
MARY: Look at me.
DIANE: I've got to hurry.
MARY: Harry always waits.
DIANE: He said he's got something on his mind.
MARY: You've got the luck.
(*Pause.*)
MARY: Look at me a second.
DIANE: All right.
(MARY *performs an aggressive curtsy.*)
MARY: Give me some advice.
DIANE: Everybody has their points.
MARY: What are my points?
DIANE: What are your points?
MARY: Name my points.
(MARY *stands there belligerently. She lifts up her skirt. She rolls up her sleeves. She tucks her sweater in tight.*)
DIANE: I've got to hurry.
MARY: Name one point.
DIANE: You've got nice hands.
MARY (*Surprised*): Do I?
DIANE: Very nice hands.
MARY: Do I really?
DIANE: Hands are very important.
(MARY *shows her hands to the mirror and gives them little exercises.*)

DIANE: Men often look at hands.
MARY: They do?
DIANE: Often.
MARY: What do they think?
DIANE: Think?
MARY (*Impatiently*): When they look at hands.
DIANE: They think: There's a nice pair of hands.
MARY: What else?
DIANE: They think: Those are nice hands to hold.
MARY: And?
DIANE: They think: Those are nice hands to – squeeze.
MARY: I'm listening.
DIANE: They think: Those are nice hands to – kiss.
MARY: Go on.
DIANE: They think – (*racking her brain for compassion's sake.*)
MARY: Well?
DIANE: Those are nice hands to – love!
MARY: Love!
DIANE: Yes.
MARY: What do you mean "love"?
DIANE: I don't have to explain.
MARY: Someone is going to love my hands?
DIANE: Yes.
MARY: What about my arms?
DIANE: What about them? (*A little surly.*)
MARY: Are they one of my points?
(*Pause.*)
DIANE: I suppose not one of your best.
MARY: What about my shoulders?
(*Pause.*)
DIANE: Your shoulders are all right.
MARY: You know they're not. They're not.
DIANE: Then what did you ask me for?
MARY: What about my bosom?
DIANE: I don't know your bosom.
MARY: You do know my bosom.
DIANE: I don't.
MARY: You do.
DIANE: I do not know your bosom.
MARY: You've seen me undressed.

DIANE: I never looked that hard.
MARY: You know my bosom all right. (*But she'll let it pass. She looks disgustedly at her hands.*)
MARY: Hands!
DIANE: Don't be so hard on yourself.
MARY: Sexiest knuckles on the block.
DIANE: Why hurt yourself?
MARY: My fingers are really stacked.
DIANE: Stop, sweetie.
MARY: They come when they shake hands with me.
DIANE: Now please!
MARY: You don't know how it feels.
(*Pause.*)
MARY: Just tell me what it's like.
DIANE: What like?
MARY: To be beautiful. You've never told me.
DIANE: There's no such thing as beautiful.
MARY: Sure.
DIANE: It's how you feel.
MARY: I'm going to believe that.
DIANE: It's how you feel makes you beautiful.
MARY: Do you know how I feel?
DIANE: Don't tell me.
MARY: Ugly.
DIANE: You don't have to talk like that.
MARY: I feel ugly. What does that make me?
(DIANE *declines to answer. She steps into her high heeled shoes, the elevation bringing out the harder lines of her legs, adding to her stature an appealing haughtiness and to her general beauty a touch of violence.*)
MARY: According to what you said.
DIANE: I don't know.
MARY: You said: It's how you feel makes you beautiful.
DIANE: I know what I said.
MARY: I feel ugly. So what does that make me?
DIANE: I don't know.
MARY: According to what you said.
DIANE: I don't know.
MARY: Don't be afraid to say it.
DIANE: Harry will be here.

MARY: Say it! (*Launching herself into hysteria.*)
DIANE: I've got to get ready.
MARY: You never say it. You're afraid to say it. It won't kill you. The word won't kill you. You think it but you won't say it. When you get up in the morning you tiptoe to the bathroom. I tiptoe to the bathroom but I sound like an army. What do you think I think when I hear myself? Don't you think I know the difference? It's no secret. It's not as though there aren't any mirrors. If you only said it I wouldn't try. I don't want to try. I don't want to have to try. If you only once said I was – ugly!
(DIANE *comforts her.*)
DIANE: You're not ugly, sweetie. Nobody's ugly. Everybody can be beautiful. Your turn will come. Your man will come. He'll take you in his arms. No no no, you're not ugly. He'll teach you that you are beautiful. Then you'll know what it is. (*Cradling her.*)
MARY: Will he?
DIANE: Of course he will.
MARY: Until then?
DIANE: You've got to keep going, keep looking.
MARY: Keep up with my exercises.
DIANE: Yes.
MARY: Keep up with my ballet lessons.
DIANE: Exactly.
MARY: Try and lose weight.
DIANE: Follow the book.
MARY: Brush my hair the right way.
DIANE: That's the spirit.
MARY: A hundred strokes.
DIANE: Good.
MARY: I've got to gain confidence.
DIANE: You will.
MARY: I can't give up.
DIANE: It's easier than you think.
MARY: Concentrate on my best points.
DIANE: Make the best of what you have.
MARY: Why not start now?
DIANE: **Why not.**

(MARY *gathers herself together, checks her posture in the mirror, crosses to the record-player and switches it on. "The Dance of the Sugar Plum Fairies." She begins the ballet exercises she has learned, perhaps, at the YWCA, two evenings a week. Between the final touches of her toilet* DIANE *encourages her with nods of approval. The door bell rings. Enter* HARRY *in evening clothes, glittering although his expression is solemn, for he has come on an important mission.*)

HARRY: Hi girls. Don't mind me, Mary.

(MARY *waves in the midst of a difficult contortion.*)

DIANE: Darling!

(DIANE *sweeps into his arms, takes the attitude of a dancing partner.* HARRY, *with a trace of reluctance, consents to lead her in a ballroom step across the floor.*)

HARRY: I've got something on my mind.

(DIANE *squeezes his arm, disengages herself, crosses to* MARY *and whispers.*)

DIANE: He's got something on his mind.

(DIANE *and* MARY *embrace in the usual squeaky conspiratorial manner with which girls preface happy matrimonial news. While* MARY *smiles benignly exeunt* HARRY *and* DIANE. MARY *turns the machine louder, moves in front of the mirror, resumes the ballet exercises. She stops them from time to time to check various parts of her anatomy in the mirror at close range, as if the effects of the discipline might be already apparent.*)

MARY: Goody.

(*A long determined ring of the doorbell.* MARY *stops, eyes bright with expectation. Perhaps the miracle is about to unfold. She smoothes her dress and hair, switches off the machine, opens the door. The* COLLECTOR *enters with lumbering difficulty, looks around, takes control. The power she radiates is somehow guaranteed by her grotesque form. Her body is a huge damaged tank operating under the intimate command of a brilliant field warrior which is her mind:* MARY *waits, appalled and intimidated.*)

COLLECTOR: I knew there was people in because I heard music. (MARY *cannot speak*.) Some people don't like to open the door. I'm in charge of the whole block.
MARY (*recovering*): Are you collecting for something?
COLLECTOR: The United Fund for the Obese, you know, UFO. That includes The Obese Catholic Drive, The Committee for Jewish Fat People, the Help the Blind Obese, and the Universal Aid to the Obese. If you make one donation you won't be bothered again.
MARY: We've never been asked before.
COLLECTOR: I know. But I have your card now. The whole Fund has been reorganized.
MARY: It has?
COLLECTOR: Oh yes. Actually it was my idea to have the Obese themselves go out and canvass. They were against it at first but I convinced them. It's the only fair way. Gives the public an opportunity to see exactly where their money goes. And I've managed to get the Spastic and Polio and Cancer people to see the light. It's the only fair way. We're all over the neighbourhood.
MARY: It's very – courageous.
COLLECTOR: That's what my husband says.
MARY: Your husband!
COLLECTOR: He'd prefer me to stay at home. Doesn't believe in married girls working.
MARY: Have – have you been married long?
COLLECTOR: Just short of a year. (*Coyly*.) You might say we're still honeymooners.
MARY: Oh.
COLLECTOR: Don't be embarrassed. One of the aims of our organization is to help people like me lead normal lives. Now what could be more normal than marriage? Can you think of anything more normal? Of course you can't. It makes you feel less isolated, part of the whole community. Our people are getting married all the time.
MARY: Of course, of course. (*She is disintegrating*.)
COLLECTOR: I didn't think it would work out myself at first. But John is so loving. He's taken such patience with me. When we're together it's as though there's nothing

	wrong with me at all.
MARY:	What does your husband do?
COLLECTOR:	He's a chef.
MARY:	A chef.
COLLECTOR:	Not in any famous restaurant. Just an ordinary chef. But it's good enough for me. Sometimes, when he's joking, he says I married him for his profession. (MARY *tries to laugh*.) Well I've been chatting too long about myself and I have the rest of this block to cover. How much do you think you'd like to give. I know you're a working girl.
MARY:	I don't know, I really don't know.
COLLECTOR:	May I make a suggestion?
MARY:	Of course.
COLLECTOR:	Two dollars.
MARY:	Two dollars. (*Goes to her purse obediently*.)
COLLECTOR:	I don't think that's too much, do you?
MARY:	No no.
COLLECTOR:	Five dollars would be too much.
MARY:	Too much.
COLLECTOR:	And one dollar just doesn't seem right.
MARY:	Oh, I only have a five. I don't have any change.
COLLECTOR:	I'll take it.
MARY:	You'll take it?
COLLECTOR:	I'll take it. (*A command*.)

(MARY *drops the bill in the transaction, being afraid to make any physical contact with the* COLLECTOR. MARY *stoops to pick it up. The* COLLECTOR *prevents her*.)

COLLECTOR:	Let me do that. The whole idea is not to treat us like invalids. You just watch how well I get along.

(*The* COLLECTOR *retrieves the money with immense difficulty*.)

COLLECTOR:	That wasn't so bad, was it?
MARY:	No. Oh no. It wasn't so bad.
COLLECTOR:	I've even done a little dancing in my time.
MARY:	That's nice.
COLLECTOR:	They have courses for us. First we do it in water, but very soon we're right up there on dry land. I bet you do some dancing yourself, a girl like you. I heard music when I came.

MARY: Not really.
COLLECTOR: Do you know what would make me very happy?
MARY: It's very late.
COLLECTOR: To see you do a step or two.
MARY: I'm quite tired.
COLLECTOR: A little whirl.
MARY: I'm not very good.
COLLECTOR: A whirl, a twirl, a bit of a swing. I'll put it on for you.
(*The* COLLECTOR *begins to make her way to the record-player.* MARY, *who cannot bear to see her expend herself, overtakes her and switches it on.* MARY *performs for a few moments while the* COLLECTOR *looks on with pleasure, tapping out the time.* MARY *breaks off the dance.*)
MARY: I'm not very good.
COLLECTOR: Would a little criticism hurt you?
MARY: No –
COLLECTOR: They're not dancing like that any more.
MARY: No?
COLLECTOR: They're doing something altogether different.
MARY: I wouldn't know.
COLLECTOR: More like this.
(*The record has reached the end of its spiral and is now jerking back and forth over the last few bars.*)
COLLECTOR: Don't worry about that.
(*The* COLLECTOR *moves to stage centre and executes a terrifying dance to the repeating bars of music. It combines the heavy mechanical efficiency of a printing machine with the convulsions of a spastic. It could be a garbage heap falling down an escalator. It is grotesque but military, excruciating but triumphant. It is a woman-creature proclaiming a disease of the flesh.* MARY *tries to look away but cannot. She stares, dumbfounded, shattered, and ashamed.*)
COLLECTOR: We learn to get around, don't we?
MARY: It's very nice. (*She switches off the machine.*)
COLLECTOR: That's more what they're doing.
MARY: Is it?
COLLECTOR: In most of the places. A few haven't caught on.

MARY: I'm very tired now. I think –
COLLECTOR: You must be tired.
MARY: I am.
COLLECTOR: With all my talking.
MARY: Not really.
COLLECTOR: I've taken your time.
MARY: You haven't.
COLLECTOR: I'll write you a receipt.
MARY: It isn't necessary.
COLLECTOR: Yes it is. (*She writes*.) This isn't official. An official receipt will be mailed to you from Fund headquarters. You'll need it for Income Tax.
MARY: Thank you.
COLLECTOR: Thank *you*. I've certainly enjoyed this.
MARY: Me too. (*She is now confirmed in a state of numbed surrender*.)
COLLECTOR (*with a sudden disarming tenderness that changes through the speech into a vision of uncompromising domination*): No, you didn't. Oh, I know you didn't. It frightened you. It made you sort of sick. It had to frighten you. It always does at the beginning. Everyone is frightened at the beginning. That's part of it. Frightened and – fascinated. Fascinated – that's the important thing. You were fascinated too, and that's why I know you'll learn the new step. You see, it's a way to start over and forget about all the things you were never really good at. Nobody can resist that, can they? That's why you'll learn the new step. That's why I must teach you. And soon you'll want to learn. Everybody will want to learn. We'll be teaching everybody.
MARY: I'm fairly busy.
COLLECTOR: Don't worry about that. We'll find time. We'll make time. You won't believe this now, but soon, and it will be very soon, you're going to want me to teach you everything. Well, you better get some sleep. Sleep is very important. I want to say thank you. All the Obese want to say thank you.
MARY: Nothing. Goodnight.
COLLECTOR: Just beginning for us.
(*Exit the* COLLECTOR. MARY, *dazed and exhausted*,

stands at the door for some time. She moves toward stage centre, attempts a few elementary exercises, collapses into the chair and stares dumbly at the audience. The sound of a key in the lock. Door opens. Enter DIANE *alone, crying.*)

DIANE: I didn't want him to see me home.
(MARY *is unable to cope with anyone else's problem at this point.*)
MARY: What's the matter with you?
DIANE: It's impossible.
MARY: What's impossible?
DIANE: What happened.
MARY: What happened?
DIANE: He doesn't want to see me any more.
MARY: Harry?
DIANE: Harry.
MARY: Your Harry?
DIANE: You know damn well which Harry.
MARY: Doesn't want to see you any more?
DIANE: No.
MARY: I thought he loved you.
DIANE: So did I.
MARY: I thought he really loved you.
DIANE: So did I.
MARY: You told me he said he loved you.
DIANE: He did.
MARY: But now he doesn't?
DIANE: No.
MARY: Oh.
DIANE: It's terrible.
MARY: It must be.
DIANE: It came so suddenly.
MARY: It must have.
DIANE: I thought he loved me.
MARY: So did I.
DIANE: He doesn't!
MARY: Don't cry.
DIANE: He's getting married.
MARY: He isn't!
DIANE: Yes.
MARY: He isn't!

DIANE: This Sunday.
MARY: This Sunday?
DIANE: Yes.
MARY: So soon?
DIANE: Yes.
MARY: He told you that?
DIANE: Tonight.
MARY: What did he say?
DIANE: He said he's getting married this Sunday.
MARY: He's a bastard.
DIANE: Don't say that.
MARY: I say he's a bastard.
DIANE: Don't talk that way.
MARY: Why not?
DIANE: Don't.
MARY: After what he's done?
DIANE: It's not his fault.
MARY: Not his fault?
DIANE: He fell in love.
(*The word has its magic effect.*)
MARY: Fell in *love*?
DIANE: Yes.
MARY: With someone else?
DIANE: Yes.
MARY: He fell out of love with you?
DIANE: I suppose so.
MARY: That's terrible.
DIANE: He said he couldn't help it.
MARY: Not if it's love.
DIANE: He said it was.
MARY: Then he couldn't help it.
(DIANE *begins to remove her make-up and undress, reversing exactly every step of her toilet.* MARY, *still bewildered, but out of habit, assists her.*)
MARY: And you're so beautiful.
DIANE: No.
MARY: Your hair.
DIANE: No.
MARY: Your shoulders.
DIANE: No.
MARY: Everything.

>   (*Pause.*)
> MARY: What did he say?
> DIANE: He told me everything.
> MARY: Such as what?
> DIANE: Harry's a gentleman.
> MARY: I always thought so.
> DIANE: He wanted me to know everything.
> MARY: It's only fair.
> DIANE: He told me about her.
> MARY: What did he say?
> DIANE: He said he loves her.
> MARY: Then he had no choice.
> DIANE: He said she's beautiful.
> MARY: He didn't!
> DIANE: What can you expect?
> MARY: I suppose so.
> DIANE: He loves her, after all.
> MARY: Then I guess he thinks she's beautiful.
>   (*Pause.*)
> MARY: What else did he say?
> DIANE: He told me everything.
> MARY: How did he meet her?
> DIANE: She came to his house.
> MARY: What for?
> DIANE: She was collecting money.
> MARY: Money! (*Alarm.*)
> DIANE: For a charity.
> MARY: Charity!
> DIANE: Invalids of some kind.
> MARY: Invalids!
> DIANE: That's the worst part.
> MARY: What part?
> DIANE: She's that way herself.
> MARY: What way?
> DIANE: You know.
> MARY: What way, what way?
> DIANE: You know.
> MARY: Say it!
> DIANE: She's an invalid.
> MARY: Harry's marrying an invalid?
> DIANE: This Sunday.

MARY: You said he said she was beautiful.
DIANE: He did.
MARY: Harry is going to marry an invalid.
DIANE: What should I do?
MARY: Harry who said he loved you. (*Not a question.*)
DIANE: I'm miserable.
(MARY *is like a woman moving through a fog toward a light.*)
MARY: Harry is going to marry an invalid. He thinks she's beautiful.
(MARY *switches on the record-player.*) She came to his door. Harry who told you he loved you. You who told me I had my points.
(*"The Dance of the Sugar-Plum Fairies" begins.* MARY *dances but she does not use the steps she learned at the* YWCA. *She dances in conscious imitation of the* COLLECTOR.)
DIANE: What are you doing? (*Horrified.*)
(MARY *smiles at her.*)
DIANE: Stop it! Stop it this instant!
MARY: Don't tell me what to do. Don't you dare. Don't ever tell me what to do. Don't ever.
(*The dance continues.* DIANE, *dressed in bra and panties as at the beginning, backs away.*)

CURTAIN

THE PAPER

My fingers trembled
like eyelashes assailed by lust
I signed a paper preventing
the Market from loving me
My childhood friends lined up
to say goodbye
I mistook their gesture
for a firedrill
and out of habit of hatred
for the make-believe
I underlined my signature

Goodbye girls and boys
I call today in a riper voice
In the cold mirror of opium
I saw all our lives
connected and precise
as pieces in a clock
and the shining ladder
I teetered on was nothing
but the pendulum

NURSERY RHYME

A beautiful woman dignified
the cocktail lounge
    suddenly we were drinking
for a reason
We were all Absolutists
    with a rose carved in our minds
by a 5-year-old brain surgeon
Gentlemen
somewhere a shabby wife waits for us
with some decent news about chickenpox
But let me speak for myself
I believe in God
I have seen angels pulsing
    through the veined atmosphere
I am alone with a window
    full of bones and wrinkles
O terrible eyes
O perfect mouth
    my fantasy shipwrecked
on the metal of your hair
Your beauty rides a wet flower
like a sail above a deep old hull
    I need to touch you
with my fleshy calipers
Desire is the last church
and the ashtrays
    are singing with hunger
Even if you are the Golden Calf
you are better than money
or government
    and I have bent my knee
Roses are roses
blue is blue
History Greece Art Measure Face Tree Sphere Blossom Terror Rose
remind me remind me remind me

OLD DIALOGUE

- Has this new life deepened your perceptions?
- I suppose so.
- Then you are being trained correctly.
- For what?
- If you knew we could not train you.

WINTER BULLETIN

Toronto has been good to me
I relaxed on TV
I attacked several dead horses
I spread rumours about myself
I reported a Talmudic quarrel
    with the Montreal Jewish Community
I forged a death certificate
    in case I had to disappear
I listened to a huckster
    welcome me to the world
I slept behind my new sunglasses
I abandoned the care of my pimples
I dreamed that I needed nobody
I faced my trap
I withheld my opinion on matters
    on which I had no opinion

I humoured the rare January weather
    with a jaunty step for the sake of heroism
Not very carefully
    I thought about the future
and how little I know about animals
The future seemed unnecessarily black and strong
as if it had received my casual mistakes
through a carbon sheet

WHY DID YOU GIVE MY NAME

TO THE POLICE?

You recited the Code of Comparisons
in your mother's voice.
Again you were the blue-robed seminary girl
but these were not poplar trees and nuns
you walked between.
These were Laws.
Damn you for making this moment hopeless,
now, as a clerk in uniform fills
in my father's name.

You too must find the moment hopeless
in the Tennyson Hotel.
I know your stomach.
The brass bed bearing your suitcase
rumbles away like an automatic
promenading target in a shooting gallery:
you stand with your hands full
of a necklace you wanted to pack.
In detail you recall your rich dinner.
Grab that towel rack!

Doesn't the sink seem a fraud
with its hair-swirled pipes?
Doesn't the overhead bulb
seem burdened with mucous?
Things will be better at City Hall.

Now you must learn to read
newspapers without laughing.
No hysterical headline breakfasts.
Police be your Guard,
Telephone Book your Brotherhood.
Action! Action! Action!
Goodbye Citizen.

The clerk is talking to nobody.
Do you see how I have tiptoed
out of his brown file?
He fingers his uniform
like a cheated bargain hunter.
Answer me, please talk to me, he weeps,
say I'm not a doorman.

I plug the wires of your fear
(ah, this I was always meant to do)
into the lust-asylum universe:
raped by aimless old electricity
you stiffen over the steel books of your bed
like a fish
in a liquid air experiment.
Thus withers the Civil Triumph
(Laws rush in to corset the collapse)
for you are mistress to the Mayor,
he electrocuted in your frozen juices.

GOVERNMENTS MAKE ME LONELY

Speech from the Throne
dissolves my friends
like a miracle soap
and there's only the Queen and me
and her English
Soon she's gone too
I find myself wandering
with her English
across a busy airfield
I am insignificant as an aspirant
in the Danger Reports
Why did I listen to the radio
A man with a yellow bolo-bat
lures my immortal destiny
into a feeding trough
for Royal propellers
and her English follows
like an airline shoulder bag
I'm alone
Goodbye little Jewish soul
I knew things
would not go soft for you
but I meant you
for a better wilderness

THE LISTS

Straffed by the Milky Way
vaccinated by a snarl of clouds
lobotomized by the bore of the moon
he fell in a heap
some woman's smell
smeared across his face
a plan for Social Welfare
rusting in a trouser cuff
    From five to seven
tall trees doctored him
mist roamed on guard
    Then it began again
the sun stuck a gun in his mouth
the wind started to skin him
Give up the Plan give up the Plan
echoing among its scissors
    The women who elected him
performed erotic calesthenics
above the stock-reports
of every hero's fame
    Out of the corner of his stuffed eye
etched in minor metal
under his letter of the alphabet
he clearly saw his tiny name
    Then a museum slid under
his remains like a shovel

TO THE INDIAN PILGRIMS

I am the country you meant
I am the chalk snake
    fading in the remote village
I am the smiling man
    who gave you water
I am the shoemaker
    you could not speak to
but whom you believed could love you
I am the carver of the moon-round breasts
I am the flesh teacher
I am the demon
    who laughs himself to death
I am the country you meant
As the virgin places the garland
on the soft river
    I can put a discipline
across your bellies
I do not know all my knowledge
and I know that this is my strength
I am the country
    you will love and hate
I am the policeman
    floating on Upanishads
The epidemic burns
    village after village
in a tedious daily fire
The white doctors sweat
the black doctors sweat
I am the epidemic
I am the teacher
    whom the teachers hate
I am the country you meant
I am the snake beaten out of silver
I am the black ornament
The ivory bridge
    leaps over the thick stream
I bring it down with a joke
I whistle it into ruins
The sunlight gnaws at it
The moonlight gives it leprosy

I am the agent
I am the disease
The world stiffens suddenly
and gravity sinks its teeth
    into village balloons
and water injures the red of blood
and pebbles surrender
    their rough little mouths
and you secret loving names
turn up in dossiers
when I show in black and white
    exactly where your thumbs
and tickets aim

THE MUSIC CREPT BY US

I would like to remind
the management
that the drinks are watered
and the hat-check girl
has syphilis
and the band is composed
of former SS monsters
However since it is
New Year's Eve
and I have lip cancer
I will place my
paper hat on my
concussion and dance

THE TELEPHONE

Mother, the telephone is ringing in the empty house.
It rang all Wednesday
    Sometimes the people next door thought it was their phone,
A rusty sound, if ringing has a colour
as if, whatever the message, it would be obsolete,
news already acted on, or ignored
                like an anecdote about McCarthy or
the insurance man about the cheque which has already been mailed.
or a wedding of old people
    Did we ever use these battered pots, I wondered once
while rummaging in the basement. We must have been poor
or deliberately austere, but I was not told.
    A rusty sound, a touch of violence in it
rather than urgency, as if the message demanded a last resource
from the instrument.
                Harbour of floating incidental information
our telephone was feminine
an ugly girl who had cultivated a good nature
slightly promiscuous
              A rusty sound, like the old girl,
never "fatale," trying to spread for a childhood chum
just for auld lang syne.
Mother, someone is trying to get through,
probably to remind you of Daylight Saving Time
    Someone must compose your number
to remind you of Daylight Saving Time
even though you've changed all the clocks you can reach
Answer the phone, dust
Answer the phone, plastic Message-Riter
    Answer the phone, darlings who lived in the house
even before us
    Answer the phone, another family
Someone wants to say hello about nothing
Answer the phone, you who followed your career
past the comfort of gossip

                      who listen to the banal regular ringing
and give your venom to it
enforce it with your hatred
until the walls are marked by its dentist's persistence
like a negro's house
                      with obscenities and crosses
You are a little boy
lying in bed in the early summer
    the telephone is ringing
    your parents are in the garden
and they rush to get it
before it wakes you up
                    you who used your boyhood as a discipline
against the profane –
                    your moulding discipline
you : single, awake, contemptuous even of exile
Your parents rush to stop the ringing
    which would let you rejoice in Daylight Saving Time
or how the project is coming along
and you shall not alter your love
assailed as it is by your nature, your insight,
Time or the World,
though the ringing brocade your contempt like a royal garment
you shall set aside a hiding place
you shall not alter your love

DISGUISES

I am sorry that the rich man must go
and his house become a hospital.
I loved his wine, his contemptuous servants,
his ten-year-old ceremonies.
I loved his car which he wore like a snail's shell
everywhere, and I loved his wife,
the hours she put into her skin,
the milk, the lust, the industries
that served her complexion.
I loved his son who looked British
but had American ambitions
and let the word aristocrat comfort him
like a reprieve while Kennedy reigned.
I loved the rich man : I hate to see
his season ticket for the Opera
fall into a pool for opera-lovers.

I am sorry that the old worker must go
who called me mister when I was twelve
and sir when I was twenty
who studied against me in obscure socialist
clubs which met in restaurants.
I loved the machine he knew like a wife's body.
I loved his wife who trained bankers
in an underground pantry
and never wasted her ambition in ceramics.
I loved his children who debate
and come first at McGill University.
Goodbye old gold-watch winner
all your complex loyalties
must now be borne by one-faced patriots.

Goodbye dope fiends of North Eastern Lunch
circa 1948, your spoons which were not
Swedish Stainless, were the same colour
as the hoarded clasps and hooks
of discarded soiled therapeutic corsets.
I loved your puns about snow
even if they lasted the full seven-month
Montreal winter. Go write your memoirs
for the Psychedelic Review.

Goodbye sex fiends of Beaver Pond
who dreamed of being jacked-off
by electric milking machines.
You had no Canada Council.
You had to open little boys
with a pen-knife.
I loved your statement to the press:
"I didn't think he'd mind."
Goodbye articulate monsters
Abbot and Costello have met Frankenstein.

I am sorry that the conspirators must go
the ones who scared me by showing me
a list of all the members of my family.
I loved the way they reserved judgement
about Genghis Khan. They loved me because
I told them their little beards
made them dead-ringers for Lenin.
The bombs went off in Westmount
and now they are ashamed
like a successful outspoken Schopenhauerian
whose room-mate has committed suicide.
Suddenly they are all making movies.
I have no one to buy coffee for.

I embrace the changeless:
the committed men in public wards
oblivious as Hassidim
who believe that they are someone else.
Bravo! Abelard, viva! Rockefeller,
have these buns, Napoleon,
hurrah! betrayed Duchess.
Long live you chronic self-abusers!
you monotheists!
you familiars of the Absolute
sucking at circles!
You are all my comfort
as I turn to face the beehive
as I disgrace my style
as I coarsen my nature
as I invent jokes
as I pull up my garters
as I accept responsibility.

You comfort me
incorrigible betrayers of the self
as I salute fashion
and bring my mind
    like a promiscuous air-hostess
handing out parachutes in a nose dive
bring my butchered mind
to bear upon the facts.

LOT

Give me back my house
Give me back my young wife
    I shouted to the sunflower in my path
Give me back my scalpel
Give me back my mountain view
    I said to the seeds along my path
Give me back my name
Give me back my childhood list
    I whispered to the dust when the path gave out
Now sing
Now sing
    sang my master as I waited in the raw wind
Have I come so far for this
    I wondered as I waited in the pure cold
    ready at last to argue for my silence
Tell me master
do my lips move
or where does it come from
    this soft total chant that drives my soul
    like a spear of salt into the rock
Give me back my house
Give me back my young wife

ONE OF THE NIGHTS I

DIDN'T KILL MYSELF

You dance on the day you saved
my theoretical angels
daughters of the new middle-class
who wear your mouths like Bardot
    Come my darlings
the movies are true
I am the lost sweet singer whose death
in the fog your new high-heeled boots
have ground into cigarette butts
I was walking the harbour this evening
looking for a 25-cent bed of water
but I will sleep tonight
with your garters curled in my shoes
like rainbows on vacation
with your virginity ruling
the condom cemeteries like a 2nd chance
I believe I believe
Thursday December 12th
is not the night
and I will kiss again the slope of a breast
little nipple above me
like a sunset

THE BIG WORLD

The big world will find out
about this farm
the big world will learn
the details of what
I worked out in the can

And your curious life with me
will be told so often
that no one will believe
you grew old

NARCISSUS

You don't know anyone
You know some streets
hills, gates, restaurants
The waitresses have changed

You don't know me
I'm happy about the autumn
the leaves the red skirts
everything moving

I passed you in a marble wall
some new bank
You were bleeding from the mouth
You didn't even know the season

CHERRY ORCHARDS

Canada some wars are waiting for you
some threats
some torn flags
Inheritance is not enough
    Faces must be forged under the hammer
of savage ideas
    Mailboxes will explode
in the cherry orchards
and somebody will wait forever
for his grandfather's fat cheque
    From my deep café I survey the quiet snowfields
like a u.s. promoter
of a new plastic snowshoe
looking for a moving speck
a troika perhaps
an exile
an icy prophet
an Indian insurrection
a burning weather station
    There's a story out there boys
Canada could you bear some folk songs
about freedom and death

STREETCARS

Did you see the streetcars
passing as of old
along Ste Catherine Street?
Golden streetcars
passing under the tearful
Temple of the Heart
where the crutches hang
like catatonic divining twigs.
A thin young priest
folds his semen in a kleenex
his face glowing
in the passing gold
as the world returns.
A lovely riot gathers the citizenry
into its spasms
as the past comes back
in the form of golden streetcars.
I carry a banner:
"The Past is Perfect"
my little female cousin
who does not believe
in our religious destiny
rides royally on my nostalgia.
The streetcars curtsy
round a corner
Firecrackers and moths
drip from their humble wires.

BULLETS

Listen all you bullets
that never hit:
a lot of throats are growing
in open collars
like frozen milk bottles
on a 5 a.m. street
throats that are waiting
for bite scars
but will settle
for bullet holes

You restless bullets
lost in swarms
from undecided wars:
fasten on
these nude throats
that need some
decoration

I've done my own work:
I had 3 jewels
no more
and I have placed them
on my choices
jewels
although they performed
like bullets:
an instant of ruby
before the hands
came up
to stem the mess

And you over there
my little acrobat:
swing fast
After me
there is no care
and the air
is heavily armed
and has
the wildest aim

HITLER

Now let him go to sleep with history,
the real skeleton stinking of gasoline,
the mutt and jeff henchmen beside him:
let them sleep among our precious poppies.

Cadres of SS waken in our minds
where they began before we ransomed them
to that actual empty realm we people
with the shadows that disturb our inward peace.

For a while we resist the silver-black cars
rolling in slow parade through the brain.
We stuff the microphones with old chaotic flowers
from a bed which rapidly exhausts itself.

Never mind. They turn up as poppies
beside the tombs and libraries of the real world.
The leader's vast design, the tilt of his chin
seem excessively familiar to minds at peace.

FRONT LAWN

The snow was falling
over my penknife
There was a movie
in the fireplace
The apples were wrapped
in 8-year-old blonde hair
Starving and dirty
the janitor's daughter never
turned up in November
to pee from her sweet crack
on the gravel
    I'll go back one day
when my cast is off
Elm leaves are falling
over my bow and arrow
Candy is going bad
and Boy Scout calendars
are on fire
    My old mother
sits in her Cadillac
laughing her Danube laugh
as I tell her that we own
all the worms
under our front lawn
    Rust rust rust
in the engines of love and time

KERENSKY

My friend walks through our city this winter night,
fur-hatted, whistling, anti-mediterranean,
stricken with seeing Eternity in all that is seasonal.
He is the Kerensky of our Circle
always about to chair the last official meeting
before the pros take over, they of the pure smiling eyes
trained only for Form.
    He knows there are no measures to guarantee
the Revolution, or to preserve the row of muscular icicles
which will chart Winter's decline like a graph.
    There is nothing for him to do but preside
over the last official meeting.
It will all come round again : the heartsick teachers
who make too much of poetry, their students
who refuse to suffer, the cache of rifles in the lawyer's attic :
and then the magic, the 80-year comet touching
the sturdiest houses. The Elite Corps commits suicide
in the tennis-ball basement. Poets ride buses free.
The General insists on a popularity poll. Troops study satire.
A strange public generosity prevails.
    Only too well he knows the tiny moment when
everything is possible, when pride is loved, beauty held
in common, like having an exquisite sister,
and a man gives away his death like a piece of advice.
    Our Kerensky has waited for these moments
over a table in a rented room
when poems grew like butterflies on the garbage of his life.
How many times? The sad answer is : they can be counted.
Possible and brief : this is his vision of Revolution.
    Who will parade the shell today? Who will kill in the name
of the husk? Who will write a Law to raise the corpse
which cries now only for weeds and excrement?
See him walk the streets, the last guard, the only idler
on the square. He must keep the wreck of the Revolution
the debris of public beauty

from the pure smiling eyes of the trained visionaries
who need our daily lives perfect.

    The soft snow begins to honour him with epaulets, and to provoke the animal past of his fur hat. He wears a death, but he allows the snow, like an ultimate answer, to forgive him, just for this jewelled moment of his coronation. The carved gargoyles of the City Hall receive the snow as bibs beneath their drooling lips. How they resemble the men of profane vision, the same greed, the same intensity as they who whip their minds to recall an ancient lucky orgasm, yes, yes, he knows that deadly concentration, they are the founders, they are the bankers – of History! He rests in his walk as they consume of the generous night everything that he does not need.

ANOTHER NIGHT WITH

TELESCOPE

Come back to me
        brutal empty room
Thin Byzantine face
    preside over this new fast
I am broken with easy grace
Let me be neither
        father nor child
but one who spins
on an eternal unimportant loom
    patterns of wars and grass
which do not last the night
        I know the stars
are wild as dust
and wait for no man's discipline
        but as they wheel
from sky to sky they rake
    our lives with pins of light